The Illustrated
Grandparent's Memories Book

Publisher and Creative Director: Nick Wells

Project Editors and Picture Research: Esme Chapman and Catherine Taylor

Art Director: Mike Spender

Special thanks to Victoria Menson.

This edition first published 2014 by

FLAME TREE PUBLISHING

Crabtree Hall, Crabtree Lane

Fulham, London SW6 6TY

United Kingdom

www.flametreepublishing.com

First published in 2014

14 16 18 17 15

1 3 5 7 9 10 8 6 4 2

© 2014 Flame Tree Publishing

ISBN 978-1-78361-297-0

Printed in China

The Illustrated
Grandparent's Memories Book

Tell The Story of Your Life

**FLAME TREE
PUBLISHING**

Contents

Introduction

amily histories are an endlessly fascinating subject. The lives of those who have gone before us shape who we are, but we don't always find out all we can. When it comes to our grandparents, we don't always think to ask questions about their lives before they had children and grandchildren, and a whole generation can be forgotten. If you can imagine the interest the early lives of your own grandparents would hold for you, you will realise how important it is to keep a record of your life to hand down to future generations; a record of not just the bare facts, but also your memories and emotions, your achievements and personality. Things that were everyday occurances for you will be fascinating to your grandchildren, and your story will enthral not only them, but one day their children and countless more generations to come.

This book provides a framework for your memories and history, asking questions that you might not have thought of, and providing plenty of space for photographs, momentoes and keepsakes. It has been designed to suit either a single grandparent or a couple, although if the latter you may prefer to each fill in a copy. However you use it, this book will become a treasure trove of family folklore and a rare insight into a personal history. Take the time to recall small details and reminisce, and the result will be a rich tapestry of enthralling family history to give to your grandchildren. Whatever the story of your life, you will be able to record it here and help to give your descendents a true flavour of who you were and the times you have lived through, something no school text book can convey quite as well.

THE CHILDHOOD YEARS

The Beginning
Brothers & Sisters
Home Life
Social Life
Schooldays

The Beginning

What is your full name?

....

Were these names chosen for a reason?

....

....

....

PLACE YOUR PHOTO HERE

PAUL LEROY
PARIS 1899

Go confidently in the direction of your dreams. Live the life you have imagined.

Henry David Thoreau

When and where were you born?

....

....

How much did you weigh at birth?

....

How old were your parents when you were born?

....

....

What's your earliest memory?

....

....

....

....

....

....

....

Brothers & Sisters

How many brothers and sisters did you have?

NAME	DATE BORN	PLACE BORN
....	....	....
....	....	....
....	....	....
....	....	....
....	....	....

PLACE YOUR PHOTO HERE

Our brothers and sisters are there with us from the dawn of our personal stories to the inevitable dusk.

Susan Scarf Merrell

Who was the best behaved?

....

....

Who was the naughtiest?

....

....

Who did you fight with and why?

....

....

....

Who did you get on well with and why?

....

....

....

What do you particularly remember about your
brothers and sisters from your childhood?

....

....

....

....

....

What were their occupations as adults?

NAME   OCCUPATION

....

....

....

....

....

PLACE YOUR PHOTO HERE

What are your memories of them in adult life?

Home Life

Where did you live when you were young?

....

....

Did you have a bedroom of your own?

....

PLACE YOUR PHOTO HERE

What do you remember about your home?

....

....

....

....

....

....

....

Where we love is home — home that our feet may leave, but not our hearts.

Oliver Wendell Holmes

Did you have a garden?

....

....

Did you move when you were young?

....

....

Where else did you live?

PLACE   DATE

....

....

....

....

What are your earliest memories?

....

....

....

What was your favourite toy?

....

....

....

What games did you play?

....

....

....

Did you have any pets?

....

....

....

*Life can only be
understood backwards;
but it must be
lived forwards.*

Søren Kierkegaard

PLACE YOUR PHOTO HERE

What were your favourite and least favourite meals?

FAVOURITE   LEAST FAVOURITE

....

....

....

....

Did you ever argue with your parents?

....

....

....

Were you given pocket money?

....

If so, how much was it?

....

Did you have to earn it?

....

....

What did you like to spend it on?

....

....

....

Did you do any chores around the house
in order to earn your pocket money?

....

....

Which was your best birthday and why was it so special?

....

....

....

....

*Life is what
happens while
you are busy
making other plans.*

John Lennon

copyright 1902
by J.G. Brown N.A.

What was the best present you ever received?

....

....

....

Did you have any family traditions at Christmas?

....

....

....

....

Do you have any special memories from other seasonal celebrations?

....

....

....

....

Social Life

Were you allowed to listen to music?

....

....

What sort of music did you like?

....

....

....

*So keep your head high,
keep your chin up, and
most importantly, keep
smiling, because life's a
beautiful thing and there's
so much to smile about.*

Marilyn Monroe

Were you allowed to wear what you wanted?

....

....

....

Who was your favourite band or musician?

....

....

....

PLACE YOUR PHOTO HERE

*Live and work but
do not forget to play,
to have fun in life
and really enjoy it.*

Eileen Caddy

Did you have a favourite
actor or actress?

....

....

....

....

Was there anywhere you used to go to regularly
in the evenings or at weekends?

....

....

....

....

Who was your first kiss with?

....

....

How old were you?

....

Who was your first boyfriend or girlfriend?

....

....

....

How long were you together?

....

....

....

The unexamined life is not worth living.

Socrates

PLACE YOUR PHOTO HERE

Schooldays

Describe your first school. How old were you when you went there?

....

....

....

....

....

....

What do you remember about your teachers? Did you like it there?

....

....

....

....

....

....

Which school did you move on to after that?

....

....

....

How did you get to school?

....

....

....

Did you have a best friend?

....

....

....

An investment in knowledge pays the best interest.

Benjamin Franklin

How did you meet them?

....

....

....

Who were your other friends?

NAMES

....

....

....

What were your favourite and least favourite subjects?

FAVOURITE   LEAST FAVOURITE

....

....

....

....

....

Who was your favourite teacher and why?

....

....

....

....

....

How much homework were you given?

....

....

....

Did you have to wear a uniform? Describe it.

....

....

....

Were you well-behaved or did you ever get into trouble at school?

....

....

....

Did you learn any musical instruments?

....

....

....

Education is the most powerful weapon which you can use to change the world.

Nelson Mandela

Were you good at sports?

....

....

....

Education is not the filling of a pail, but the lighting of a fire.

William Butler Yeats

What did you play?

....

....

....

PLACE YOUR PHOTO HERE

PLACE YOUR PHOTO HERE

Did you have a part-time or Saturday job when you were older?

....

....

How old were you when you left school?

....

Did you go on to further studies?

....

If so, where did you go and what did you study?

....

If not, what did you do?

....

What qualifications did you gain?

SUBJECT	QUALIFICATION
....	....
....	....
....	....
....	....

What are your best memories of this time?

....

....

....

....

....

....

FAMILY HISTORY

Your Family Tree
Your Parents
Your Grandparents

Your Family Tree

Family is the most important thing in the world.
Princess Diana

GRANDFATHER	GRANDMOTHER	GRANDFATHER	GRANDMOTHER
....	....	....	....

UNCLES	AUNTS	UNCLES	AUNTS
	....	....	....
....	....	....	....
....	....	....	....

FATHER	MOTHER
....	....

BROTHERS	SISTERS
....	....
....	....
....	....

YOU

....

Your Parents

What was your father's name?

....

When and where was he born?

DATE BORN   PLACE BORN

....

PLACE YOUR PHOTO HERE

What was his occupation?

....

*A father's goodness is
higher than the mountain,
a mother's goodness
deeper than the sea.*

Japanese Proverb

What were his interests and hobbies?

....

....

....

....

PLACE YOUR PHOTO HERE

What was your mother's full name before she was married?

....

When and where was she born?

DATE BORN   PLACE BORN

....

What was her occupation?

....

What were her interests and hobbies?

....

....

....

....

....

....

No matter how far we come, our parents are always in us.

Brad Meltzer

Did she continue to work after her marriage?

....

....

....

What are your fondest memories of her?

....

....

....

....

Describe your favourite memory with your parents.

....

....

....

....

Your Grandparents

What were your father's parents' names?

NAME	DATE BORN	PLACE BORN
....	....	....
....	....	....

PLACE YOUR PHOTO HERE

If nothing is going well, call your grandmother.

Italian proverb

What were their occupations?

GRANDFATHER   GRANDMOTHER

....

When did they die?

GRANDFATHER   GRANDMOTHER

....

How old were they?

GRANDFATHER   GRANDMOTHER

....

What were your mother's parents' names?

NAME	DATE BORN	PLACE BORN
....	....	....
....	....	....

What were their occupations?

GRANDFATHER   GRANDMOTHER

....

A grandfather is someone with silver in his hair and gold in his heart. Unknown

PLACE YOUR PHOTO HERE

When did they die?

GRANDFATHER

GRANDMOTHER

....

....

How old were they?

GRANDFATHER

GRANDMOTHER

....

....

Do you remember spending time with your grandparents?

....

....

....

What did you do together?

....

....

....

....

....

Nobody can do for little children what grandparents do. Grandparents sort of sprinkle stardust over the lives of little children.

Alex Haley

ADULT YEARS

Working Life
When You Met
Your Wedding
Married Life

Working Life

What was your first full-time job?

....

Did you enjoy it?

....

....

PLACE YOUR PHOTO HERE

How much were you paid?

....

Did you move to a
different place for work?

....

....

You've achieved
success in your field
when you don't know
whether what you're
doing is work or play.

Warren Beatty

Was it easy or hard
to make ends meet?

....

....

....

How did you travel to work?

....

....

Opportunity is missed by most people because it is dressed in overalls and looks like work.

Thomas Edison

To fulfill a dream, to be allowed to sweat over lonely labor, to be given a chance to create, is the meat and potatoes of life. The money is the gravy.

Bette Davis

What hours did you work?

....

What were your colleagues like?

....

....

How long did you stay in your first job?

....

Where have you worked since?

....

....

....

Where did you most enjoy working?

....

What was your main occupation during your working life?

....

What did you want to be when you were a child?

....

....

If you could do it all again, would you choose a different career?

....

....

Do you have any job advice for your grandchildren?

....

....

....

....

....

When You Met

How did you first meet your future husband or wife?

....

....

....

....

How old were you both?

....

What were your first impressions of each other?

....

....

....

....

....

....

*Love doesn't make
the world go round.
Love is what makes
the ride worthwhile.*

Franklin P. Jones

Where did you go on your first date?

....

....

....

....

When did you fall in love?

....

....

What's your favourite memory of your early days together?

....

....

....

....

....

How long were you together before you got engaged?

....

Describe the proposal.

....

....

....

....

....

....

....

....

....

> *All love stories are tales of beginnings. When we talk about falling in love, we go to the beginning, to pinpoint the moment of freefall.*
>
> *Meghan O'Rourke*

How long was your engagement?

....

....

Your Wedding

What was the date of your wedding?

....

How old were you both when you got married?

....

Where did the ceremony take place?

....

PLACE YOUR PHOTO HERE

What did you wear on your wedding day?

....

....

....

....

Who was the best man?

....

Did you have any bridesmaids?

....

....

....

A successful marriage requires falling in love many times, always with the same person.

Mignon McLaughlin

How many guests came?

....

Did you have a reception?

....

Happy is the man who finds a true friend, and far happier is he who finds that true friend in his wife.

Franz Schubert

Where was it held?

....

....

....

What did you eat?

....

....

....

....

....

Did you dance to a special song?

....

....

Did you have a band or DJ?

....

....

What are your special memories of your wedding day?

....

....

....

....

....

....

Did you receive any nice gifts?

Coming together is a beginning; keeping together is progress; working together is success.

Henry Ford

....

....

....

Did you have a honeymoon? Where did you go?

....

....

....

Married Life

Where was your first home together? Describe it.

....

....

....

....

....

....

PLACE YOUR PHOTO HERE

**Why did you choose
to live there?**

....

....

....

....

*Keep love in your
heart. A life without
it is like a sunless
garden when the
flowers are dead.*

Oscar Wilde

How long did you live there?

....

PLACE YOUR PHOTO HERE

How long did you wait before having children?

....

How many children did you have?

NAME	DATE BORN	BIRTH WEIGHT
....	....	....
....	....	....
....	....	....
....	....	....
....	....	....

What are your favourite memories from when they were small?

....

....

....

Was there anywhere you went to often on family holidays?

....

....

What are your favourite married memories?

....

....

....

Have you had any special anniversary celebrations?

....

....

....

PLACE YOUR PHOTO HERE

Two things prolong your life:
A quiet heart and a loving wife.

English Proverb

IN YOUR LIFETIME

Friends & Homes
Holidays
In Your Lifetime

Friends & Homes

Who have been your best friends during your life?

....

....

....

....

How did you meet them and get to know them?

....

....

....

....

Why do you think you get on so well?

....

....

....

The language of friendship is not words but meanings.

Henry David Thoreau

PLACE YOUR PHOTO HERE

What are the happiest memories you have of your friends?

....

....

....

....

When did you move out of your parents' house?

....

....

Can you remember all the places you have lived during your lifetime?

ADDRESS	DATE	WHO LIVED THERE

Who was your best flatmate?

Which was your favourite place to live and why?

*The ache for home
lives in all of us,
the safe place where
we can go as we are
and not be questioned.*

Maya Angelou

Holidays

What sort of holidays did you go on as a child?

....

....

....

....

....

....

PLACE YOUR PHOTO HERE

Where was your favourite place to visit as a child and why?

....

....

....

....

....

Have you been back to any of these places with your own children?

....

....

....

Was it as good as you remembered?

....

....

....

....

....

Did you go on any memorable holidays after you left school?

....

....

....

....

....

Have you ever lived in another country?

....

PLACE YOUR PHOTO HERE

Did you enjoy it?

....

Do you prefer going abroad on holiday or staying at home?

....

....

What has been your favourite place to visit as an adult and why?

....

....

....

....

Where would you like to visit that you haven't yet been to?

....

....

In Your Lifetime

Have you ever met any famous people?

....

....

....

....

....

....

Be happy for this moment. This moment is your life.

Omar Khayyan

PLACE YOUR PHOTO HERE

What were the circumstances?

....

....

....

Have you witnessed any exciting or significant historical events?

....

....

....

What have been the most important historical
events to take place in your lifetime?

....

....

....

....

Life is a succession of lessons which must be lived to be understood.

Ralph Waldo Emerson

....

....

....

Do you have any regrets?

....

....

What are you most proud of?

....

PLACE YOUR PHOTO HERE

What is the best piece of advice you ever received?

....

....

....

Which person in your life has had the best influence on you?

....

....

....

....

If you could choose any occupation for a single day,
what would it be and why?

....

....

....

....

....

THE NEXT GENERATION

Your Grandchildren

Your Grandchildren

How many grandchildren do you currently have?

NAME	AGE	DATE OF BIRTH
....	....	....
....	....	....
....	....	....
....	....	....
....	....	....

PLACE YOUR PHOTO HERE

What was the grandchild you are writing this for like as a baby?

....

....

Children are the world's most valuable resource and its best hope for the future.

John F. Kennedy

....

....

....

....

....

....

PLACE YOUR PHOTO HERE

If you could give them one piece of advice, what would it be?

....

....

....

....

....

....

What are your hopes and dreams for your grandchild?

....

....

....

....

....

....

....

....

....

....

*The future belongs
to those who believe
in the beauty of
their dreams.*

Eleanor Roosevelt

Picture Credits

Front cover Leon-Emile Caille (1836–1907), *Her Pride and Joy*, 1866, © ARTOTHEK

1 George Elgar Hicks (1824–1914), *Found*, 1874, courtesy of Christie's Images Ltd/SuperStock

3 & 145 nostalgic postcard, 1900, courtesy of SuperStock

4 Ferenc Innocent (1859–1934), *Motherly Love*, 1883, courtesy of Christie's Images Ltd/SuperStock

7 Frederic, Lord Leighton (1830–1896), *Portrait of a Girl Seated on a Rug*, courtesy of Christie's Images Ltd/SuperStock

8 Henry Jules Jean Geoffroy (1853–1924), *Back to School*, 1883, courtesy of Christie's Images Ltd/SuperStock

11 Edwin Frederick Holt (1850–1865), *Guarding Baby*, courtesy of Bridgeman Art Library, London/SuperStock

12 Paul Leroy (1860–1908), *Maternity*, 1899, courtesy of Christie's Images Ltd/SuperStock

15 Carl Wentorf (1863–1914), *The Battle*, 1900, courtesy of Christie's Images Ltd/SuperStock

16 George Elgar (824–1914), *The Children of Sir Hussey Vivian Hicks*, courtesy of Bridgeman Art Library, London/SuperStock

19 Jozef Israels (1824–1911), *Children Playing By The Seaside*, courtesy of Christie's Images Ltd/SuperStock

20 Federica Giuseppina Gervasoni Giuliano (1838–1915), *Returning Home From Working in The Fields*, 1863, courtesy of Universal Images Group/Superstock

23 Carlton Alfred Smith (1853–1946), *The Spoilt Child*, 1899, courtesy of Christie's Images Ltd/SuperStock

25 Hermann Seeger (1857–1920), *Summer's Delight*, 1899, courtesy of Christie's Images Ltd/SuperStock

26 Elena Dmitryevna Polenova (1850–1898), *Child Room*, 1892, courtesy of Fine Art Images/SuperStock

29 John Callcott Horsley (1817–1903), *The New Dress*, courtesy of Christie's Images Ltd/SuperStock

30 Boris Michaylovich Kustodiev (1878–1927), *Family Meal*, 1906, courtesy of Fine Art Images/SuperStock

33 John George Brown (1831–1913), *Shoeshine Boy*, 1902, courtesy of Christie's Images Ltd/SuperStock

35 Artist unknown, *Girl With Dog In Front Of Christmas Tree* (nostalgic postcard), 19th century, courtesy of SuperStock

36 Eleanor E. Manly (*fl.* 1875–98), *The Little Peacemaker*, 1895, courtesy of Christie's Images Ltd/SuperStock

38–39 Antonio Ermolao Paoletti (1834–1912), *The Dance*, courtesy of Christie's Images Ltd/SuperStock

41 Francois Louis Lanfant de Metz (1814–1892), *Dressing Up*, courtesy of Christie's Images Ltd/SuperStock

42 & back cover Rene Lelong (Op. 1890–1900), *A Spring Day By The Seashore*, courtesy of Christie's Images Ltd/SuperStock

45 John Everett Millais (1829–96), *The Woodman's Daughter*, 1850–51, courtesy of DeAgostini/SuperStock